JERICHO TUMBLING WALLS

The Story of Joshua and the Battle of Jericho
Joshua 3:1–4:24; 5:13–6:20 for children

Written by Joan E. Curren   Illustrated by Steve Edwards

Arch® Books
Copyright © 2001 Concordia Publishing House
3558 S. Jefferson Avenue, St. Louis, MO 63118-3968
Manufactured in Colombia

The Israelites had marched for years,
Now Jericho was near,
But Jordan River barred their way.
God spoke in Joshua's ear.

"The priests must bear My ark ahead,
Into the water wade.
The stream will STOP, then all can cross
On dry land, unafraid.

"Choose 12 strong men to bring 12 rocks,
From riverbed now dry.
Build an altar so all will know,
This miracle is why."

The news raced fast through Jericho.
God's miracle was clear.
The people shook and cried out loud.
Their hearts were filled with fear.

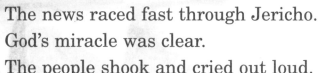

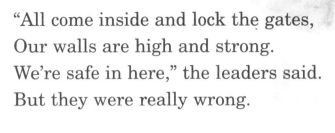

"All come inside and lock the gates,
Our walls are high and strong.
We're safe in here," the leaders said.
But they were really wrong.

The lookouts on the city walls
Yelled, "ISRAELITES IN SIGHT!"
They called the king, grabbed spears and swords,
And all prepared to fight.

First marched God's army 'round the walls,
Then seven priests trudged by,
Each trumpeting on large rams' horns
A loud and mournful cry.

Then next in line God's sacred ark
With all His laws inside,
In golden splendor, shining bright—
They carried it with pride.

A strong rear guard followed the ark.
God's people then did tramp
In silence, once around the walls.
Then all returned to camp.

The king laughed loud, his people jeered.
But then when morning came,
The Israelites marched once again.
They came and did the same.

Six days they circled city walls
Just once and then they left.
The king and people locked inside
Made jokes and called them pests.

The seventh day dawned bright and clear.
They marched 'round city walls.
Not once around this time—oh, no!
But SEVEN times in all!

"Now BLAST your horns! All people SHOUT!"
Roared Joshua to this crowd.
With all their breath, priests blew their horns,
And folks yelled long and loud.

The city walls CRACKED! SHOOK! They SLID!
Big rocks dropped all around!
The king and many people died
When the walls came tumbling down!

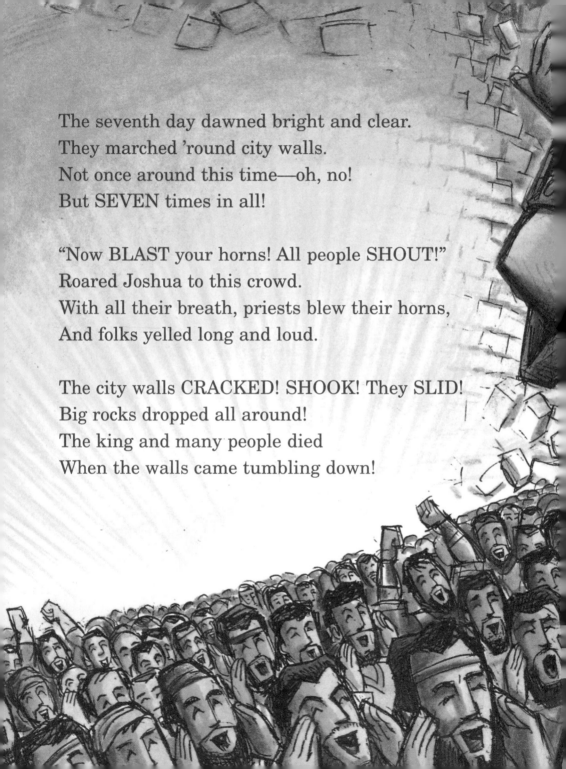

The Israelites now owned the town
And all the treasures there.
God's every word they had obeyed—
His love they did declare.

When you have problems, fear, or doubt,
Just bow your head and pray
To God who owns the victory—
He'll help you every day.

Dear Parents:

The drama of this story makes it a popular one to roleplay. It's fun to build a wall with blocks, knock it over, and watch the walls come tumbling down.

What trust Joshua and God's people displayed! The city of Jericho was a fortress. They could easily have thought that God's plan was too simple. They could have let fear overcome them and thought that they should do more to fight. But God prevailed, and they trusted. The victory was theirs because of God.

We fight the strong enemy of sin each day, and God's plan for victory is simple. We can trust and believe that the victory is ours through the death and resurrection of Jesus—pure and simple.

Find some blocks and have your family build the walls of Jericho. As you add blocks to the wall, name sins that are your enemies. Then knock over the wall and say, "The victory is ours through Jesus!" Because of Jesus, the walls of sin come tumbling down.

The Editor